Reverend Dr. Anthony Jones

Teaching in God's Kingdom

"Study to show thyself approved unto God, a workman that needeth not to be ashamed, rightly dividing the word of truth." (2 Timothy 2:15)

Reverend Dr. Anthony Jones

DORINU PUBLICATIONS, LLC

Published by DoriNu Publications, LLC

DoriNu Publications, LLC
Dayton, OH
DorindaDENusum.com

ISBN-13: 978-0-9835662-0-5

Printed in the United States of America

ENDORSEMENT

Reverend Anthony Jones' book, *Teaching As A Ministry*, is an essential tool for anyone who is entering the ministerial profession. Jones has carefully laid out a detailed guide to assist one in understanding religious concepts, the need for relationship building, spiritual teaching methodology, the challenges one would face within the industry and more! Reverend Jones' book is a true testament of his extensive knowledge of ministry and is a selfless instrument for which one can assist Jones in his quest to educate others on the proper techniques associated with soul-winning. *Teaching As A Ministry* is a reader-friendly must have!

-Dorinda D. E. Nusum, Author of *Afflicted*

Table of Contents

Preface

I am very excited for the opportunity to share with you the importance of <u>Teaching in God's Kingdom</u>. 2 Timothy 2:15 states, "Study to show thyself approved unto God, a workman that needeth not to be ashamed, rightly diving the word of truth." How can we teach the word of God unless we have been chosen, prepared, and are studying and receiving the understanding from God? Included in this book is a collection of information that I have written and received from many conferences and seminars. In order for us to meet the needs of our fellow Christians in the 21st century, there are some adjustments that we will need to make. Many of us are reluctant to change. In many cases, we want to continue doing what we have done for some 20 to 50 years. We must be willing to make the transition to changes in teaching styles, studying habits, and presentations. However, if we as Christians are unwilling to change, the world is waiting with open arms to receive our brothers and sisters with open arms. The goal of the book is to help those entering ministry to successfully build off a strong teaching foundation.

Acknowledgements

First, I have to give God all the praise, glory, and credit for all He has and is doing through me. God placed this on my heart to write this book and has given me the strength and courage to continue. To my parents and grandparents, for giving me a strong and nurturing Christian foundation. To my wife, for understanding and supporting the vision God has laid on my heart for the book. To my Pastor, Reverend Airon Reynolds Jr., for encouraging me to go forward. To Reverend Dr. Michael Bell, for encouraging and inspiring me for the last three years. To my church family, for supporting the new ideas that have been rolled out. Finally, thanks to you who saw the importance of purchasing this book for Kingdom building.

Teaching as a Ministry

Scriptures of the Old and New Testaments provide ample evidence that God's people are called to engage in the important ministry of teaching. Teachers and all who are concerned about the teaching ministry of the church could spend a very profitable time reading, studying, and interpreting some key passages that express the importance of teaching:

And these words which I command thee this day, shall be in thine heart; And thou shalt teach them diligently unto thy children, and shalt talk of them when thou sittest in thine house, and when thou walkest by the way, and when thou liest down, and when thou risest up. **(Deuteronomy 6:6,7). Read all of Deuteronomy 6:1-9.**

We will not hide them from their children, showing to the generation to come the praises of the Lord, and his strength, and his wonderful works that he hath done. **(Psalm 78:4). Read Psalm 78:1-7.**

The same day went Jesus out of the house, and sat by the sea side. And great multitudes were gathered together unto him, so that he went into a ship, and sat; and the whole multitude stood on the shore; And he spake many things unto them in parables, saying, Behold, a sower went forth to sow. **(Matthew 13:1,3). Read Matthew 13:1-58.**

Go ye therefore, and teach all nations, baptizing them in the name of the Father, and of the Son, and of the Holy Ghost. **(Matthew 28: 19-20). Read Matthew 28:1-20.**

These passages and many others emphasize the importance of relationships between those teaching and those being taught; especially the relationship of both teacher and learner to God.

Teaching

What is teaching?

Teaching is creating an experience in which a person changes in some lasting way his or her knowledge, understanding, skill, attitudes or values. Teaching involves an exchange of ideas, information, and experiences, which lead to change. Teaching utilizes environment and equipment to facilitate the experience of the learner. Keep in mind that it is better to say I don't know and I will get back to you rather than make up something and lead a person the wrong way.

What teaching is not?

Christian teaching is not coercive, it is persuasive. Coercive- to dominate and compel forcibly. Persuasive- to cause to do or act by reasoning. A person is allowed to choose. Christian learning is marked by a decision, and exercising of the will, on the part of the learner to make a change in his or her life.

Advantages of Christian teaching?

1)   Teachers are in partnership with God to bring about a change in the lives of learners.

2)   Christian teachers do not coerce learning, we should be creating an environment conducive to learning.

3)   Christian teachers do not really cause the change to take place when a person learns, we simply create an experience in which learning(change) can occur.

As Christian teachers, we should be prepared by knowing the subject, the pupils, and the tools available for effective teaching. Though a challenging goal, the rewards are great-and eternal.

The Importance of Relationships

The essence of the Christian faith is identified by words that describe aspects of relationships with God and with other persons. When we speak of love, sin forgiveness, reconciliation, salvation, ministry, and many other important characteristics of the Christian faith, we are focusing on dimensions of our relationships with God and with others. Relationships from the foundation upon which the Christian community is built. Teachers play a vital role in the process of building relationships that ultimately build communities.

Possibilities for Building Relationships

- **When speaking to or about persons, use their names.** To address a student by name is to speak very personally and directly to the student. It will also help students to learn each other's name. Name tags, games using names, stories told by persons about their names, Polaroid photographs, with names attached, mounted on the bulletin board, roster of names, all are devices to help you and the students remember and use everyone's name. Knowing another's name is the first step in building a relationship.
- **Work at Being Friendly.** Work at relating to all students in ways that show friendliness, warmth, caring, and acceptance. It is not that we are asking them to be our friends but rather that we are presenting ourselves in such a way that the students may experience us as a friend.
- **Encourage cooperation, teamwork, and sharing.** As teachers, we can foster the building of relationships when we

plan activities that involve two or more persons working together and when we provide opportunities for small groups and individuals to share their work with the whole class.

- **Accept the ideas and feelings that are expressed.** If we encourage students to explore, think, interpret, create, and express themselves, then it is imperative that we be open to a wide variety of their expressions. A good give-and-take interaction where differences are expressed provides a potential for building relationships.

- **Spend time in personal conversation.** If the class is large and the teacher is working alone, it is impossible to spend much individual time with every member of the class during each session. However, during the course of two of three months it should be possible to engage each student in a personal conversation, either before, during, or after class. There are many ways to reach out to students for a brief conversation: *Inquire about special events in their lives, ask about members of the family, be sensitive to their moods, worries, joys, or comment on class participation, special interest, or abilities.* In whatever way we connect through conversations with the persons we teach, we are facilitating the building of relationships.

- **Share experiences outside the classroom.** Often students have a one-dimensional perception of teachers as authority figures responsible for presenting prescribed lessons. They seldom have the opportunity to experience their teacher in any role other than teacher. If you are able to make time you will discover many benefits from being with your students in places other than the classroom. Visits in the home, picnics, field trips, seasonal socials, service projects, and retreats are all examples of ways teacher and students can enhance their relationship outside the classroom.

- **Pray for your students.** Relationships under-girded by prayer have the potential to become lasting relationships.

- **Communicate with and about students.** An occasional phone call, a birthday card, a note saying they were missed, and other tokens of appreciation and remembrance add to building relationships.

The Distinction Between Christian and Secular Education

Secular Teaching

1. Deals only with the human.
2. Discusses the "here and now."
3. Human observation and interpretation are the basis of reality.
4. Focus is on money, business, etc.
- **Objective:** The secular objective is to make better, more effective, successful intelligent people.
- **Posture:** The posture of secular education is to help one fit into the world system.
- **Secular education asks what people know; not who they know**.

Christian Teaching

1. Deals with the transcendent.
2. Discuss the eternal.
3. A means of revelation.
4. Concerned with God as Creator, sustainer of all things. God guides history.
5. Concerned with things that last.
6. Superintended by the Holy Spirit. One cannot bear fruit without Him.
- **Objective:** The Christian objective aspires to transform people into the image of God.
- **Posture:** The Christian posture is to help lift one above the world; not only to inform the mind but also to renew the mind (Romans 12:2). **Christian education is interested in growing character, showing competence to live out the Christian faith as well as knowing what to teach and how to teach.**

The Challenge of Teaching

As a Christian teacher you are carrying out Christ's call: "Teaching them to observe all things whatsoever I have commanded you....." (Matthew 28:20). The teacher's task is very important for several reasons.

1. **God and teachers are partners-** members of the same team. If you were bowling on a team trying to win the league championship, you'd like to have the best bowlers in the league on your team. A person's confidence and ability are greatly strengthened when he or she is able to play, work, and team with quality persons. **You do not teach alone.** When teaching, feel good about the fact that God and you are the same team. You have every right to be confident in this partnership since the purpose of the Sunday School and the Church's ministry is rooted in God. God is the Author of all that Christian teaching is about. The focus of your teaching is the revelation of God.

2. **Teaching, according to the New Testament writer, Paul,** is equal with preaching, evangelizing, caring, and shepherding. Jesus spent most of His three years of ministry as a teacher. Assisting others to understand the meaning of the Bible, develop their faith, and apply what they believe, to everyday life, is a supreme calling, Do not minimize the task to which you believe you have been called-to be a Christian teacher.

3. **Every teacher is in a unique position to influence** others for good and for God. Much concern is expressed today over the evil forces, which are negatively influencing the lives of children, youth, and adults in our society. Christian teachers are needed

to provide positive, meaningful Christian influence in the lives of others. Influencing others is like planting seeds. When a seed is placed in soil, tremendous forces go to work to bring forth-new life, growth and fruit. Teaching is much the same. Teachers sow a variety of seeds in many kinds of soil, some of which, under the guidance of the Holy Spirit, will bring forth life, growth and fruit. **One of the teacher's tasks is to provide the best "growing' conditions for students in a limited amount of time.** Some seeds take root and grow quickly; some die. Others take a long time to emerge from the soil. Teachers not only sow seeds, but also, cultivate the plant and soil in order to increase growth possibilities. There is also weeding to be done. Plants (learners) need good gardeners (teachers) to influence their growth and development. **However, growth is ultimately the responsibility of the Holy Spirit.**

4. **It is important to consider the needs of your students** as a challenge and an opportunity to help them. Each learner has different needs; each presents his own challenge. One of the tasks of the teacher is to discover the challenge presented and respond.

5. **Personal growth is exciting, too. Each teacher is a learner.** Most teachers will tell you that the person who learns most is the teacher! Personal growth and development are extremely important and are often suggested in Scripture (Ephesians 4:15; 2 Peter 3:18). These Scriptures suggest that we are to mature in our faith and grow as persons. You will grow and change as you teach and learn.

Teaching to Change Lives

The Challenge of Teaching and What You Bring to It

The Importance of Teaching

1. You are carrying out Christ's call (Matthew 28:20)
2. God and teachers are partners.
3. Teaching is equal with preaching, evangelizing, caring, and shepherding (Eph. 4:11)
4. Teaching can influence others for good and for God
5. Teaching and teachers meets the needs of the students.
6. Personal growth, each teacher is a learner.

What Do You Bring to Teaching?

- Each person who responds to the call to be a teacher of the Gospel of Jesus Christ brings a wealth of resources and potential to the position.
- What strengths do I bring to my teaching role? What are my inadequacies?
- Some skills I bring to teaching are:
- The commitments I bring to teaching are:
- My personal faith is:
- My areas of inadequacies are:
- How will I respond to these personal teaching needs?

10 Essentials for Excellence in Teaching

The excellent teacher……………..

1. Makes himself/herself available to God (2 Timothy 2:15a).

2. Is one who is excellent in example (1 Timothy 4:12).

3. Focuses upon reaching others for Christ (2 Timothy 2:2).

4. Majors upon quality in teaching (2 Timothy 2:15b).

5. Will minister with a loving, caring heart (2 Timothy 2:24-26).

6. Prays sincerely and fervently with a believing heart (2 Timothy 2:1,8).

7. Faithfully does the fundamentals with a flair (2 Timothy 4:1,5).

8. Has a clear vision of God's will and purpose (2 Timothy 1:6-12).

9. Is willing to change, always has a degree of flexibility (2 Timothy 1:13; 3:14-17).

10. Never gives up, preserves no matter what (2 Timothy 4:7).

Introduction to Teaching Methods

In seeking to help another to learn, there are at least three
major matters that must be considered by the teacher. **First,** the
Bible and all lessons help and must be studied. **Second,** the
teacher must determine what learning he/she wants to take place
and **third,** what material will be used in order to help this learning to
take place.

However, it is at this point that the teacher may take one of the
mistakes most common among Sunday Bible Study teachers, to feel
that all is necessary is to tell the class what she has learned. The
teacher forgets that she did not learn it that way. She learned it
through study, through research, she meditated upon it; she
analyzed it. In other words, she learned it in the crucible of
experience. The class members must learn it in a similar way. How
can the teacher lead the class to discover the insights and
information and develop the attitudes that are in harmony with her
objectives?

This is where the choice of method is involved in the teacher's
preparation. The teacher must bridge the gap between her study
and the pupils learning. It is not enough for the teacher to know the
material; She must also know how to help her learners to know, to
feel, to believe, to act. To do this it is imperative that the teacher be
concerned about method in teaching.

The problem of method involved more than the choice of
specific methods. The study must have meaning for the learner; it
must "make sense" to him. Thus, method is concerned with the
following questions:

1. How can I help my class develop an interest in this study?

2. How can I help my class develop a purpose for this study?

3. How can I help my class see the meaning in this study?

Choosing a Method

In general there are six methods of teaching:

1. Discussion
2. Question and answer
3. Lecture
4. Story
5. Project
6. Role Playing

Which method is best? No one of them is the best. Each has its own place and purpose. Probably a combination of two or more is best. Method is never an end in itself. It is always a means to an end. The important thing is not that the teacher becomes proficient in lecturing, asking questions, leading a discussion, or telling a story. The important thing is that learning take place. Method is simply an instrument used by the teacher to communicate to the learner the knowledge, ideal, or truth under consideration. That which is being taught must be communicated to the learner in such a way as to give understanding, lead to acceptance and conviction, and to secure response. Thus method must always be used in harmony with the principles of teaching.

The Discussion Method

A discussion is a co-operative search for truth in seeking the solution to a problem.

A discussion is not a debate! What are some differences between a discussion and a debate?

1. A discussion expresses individual view; a debate defends a formal position which has been taken.
2. A discussion seeks new insights; a debate seeks to prove a point.
3. A discussion is a joint search for truth; a debate seeks to win an argument.
4. A discussion presents several alternatives; a debate presents only two.
5. A discussion should never become personal; a debate may.
6. A discussion is concerned with understanding other points of view, a debate is concerned with refuting points that run counter to the position one has taken.
7. A discussion has unlimited participation on the part of the class members: a debate had limited participation.
8. A discussion is informal; a debate is formal. (If debate is informal it becomes an argument.)

VALUES
1. It leads the members to become aware of and face some of the problems they need to face as Christians. Christianity is concerned with life. Life is filled with problems. Therefore, those

problems ought to be a matter of major concern for Christian teachers as they seek to help their members grow in the Christian life.

2. It enables a person to gain new information add deeper insights from the views expressed by fellow class members and the teacher.

3. It gives an individual the opportunity to study the teachings of the Bible in terms of a problem he is facing in life.

4. It gives him an opportunity to express and clarify his own views in the light of the total class discussion.

5. It gives him an opportunity to evaluate and perhaps revise his own views in the light of the total discussion.

LIMITATIONS

1. A discussion in a class may be merely aimless talk. It may not lead to a positive conclusion, and it may not lead to action when action is needed.

2. The group may not have sufficient information to engage in a discussion of a given problem.

3. The conclusion may not be correct even though the class agrees on it.

4. The time allotted for discussion may be too brief to consider properly the topic being considered.

5. At the conclusion of the discussion the class may have questions that are still unanswered. If this happens the teacher must decide: (1) whether to get more information and spend more time later in discussion, or (2) accept the unanswered questions for the time and pass on to another topic.

Reverend Dr. Anthony Jones

Question and Answer Method

The reason teachers teach is to help others learn. The wise use of effective question can be one of the best aids in this process of teaching and learning. Following are some of the principles of learning and how good questions can relate to these principles.

1. Mental activity is essential to learning. Good questions stimulate mental activity on the part of the student and may thus lead to learning.
2. Discovery, that is, leading members to gain new insight, is a vital part of learning. Questions may be used to guide the learner in this process of discovering and thus contribute to learning.
3. Problem solving is closely related to learning. A question presents a problem to the learner and invites a search for an answer or a solution.

Types of Questions:

Factual questions: It is probable that teachers use factual questions more than any other type. Such questions are designed primarily to discover what facts or information the pupil may have, or to lead to mastery of knowledge. This heading is a general one, and may be sub-divided.

1. *Definition-* This type of question asks the person to use the knowledge he has to define or explain something. Example: what is meant by the word "gospel"?
2. *Sources-* This question is concerned with where certain things may be found. Example: Where do you find the most complete

account of the birth of Jesus?

3. *Who, What, When, Where-* This is probably the most common type of factual question and one of the most important. Example: Who were the Pharisees?

4. *Classification-*These questions are designed to lead the members to organize their information or knowledge into some type of classification. Example; List the Kings of Southern Israel who were predominantly good and those who were predominantly bad.

5. *Drill or review-* These questions help the members fix firmly in their minds information they have studied. Example: Who will repeat for us the books of the Bible?

Thought Questions: These are questions designed to stimulate thought, to seek opinions, and to lead to understanding. This is also a general category and may be divided into sub-types.

1. **Stimulate thought-**These are questions that stimulate the members to think and to share their ideas and opinions with the class. This way they may be lead to new and deeper insights. Example: Is it wrong to go to a baseball game on Sunday? Why or Why not?

2. **Deepen Understanding-** Through this type of question the teacher seeks to determine the pupil's understanding in a given area. The questions dealing with understanding are generally of two types.

a). **Meaning-**This is important because teachers often assume their class members know the meaning of Scripture passage when they do not. Example" One of the Beatitudes is," Blessed are the poor in spirit." What does this mean?

b). **Relationship to life-**This type of question also involves an understanding of meaning but goes one step further. It seeks to determine whether the individual sees any relationship between the passage being studied and his present experience. Example: The Bible tells us that we should love our enemies. Can you think of any experience in your life where this verse would apply?

3. *Seek clarification-*These are questions the teacher should ask to a member to clarify his thinking. The purpose of the teacher here is not to challenge the position of the person but to make sure he believes what he thinks he believes. Example: The person says, "I believe in the complete separation of church and state." The teacher might say, "Does this mean that you would not favor having the government support chaplains in the armed forces?

Learning Activities

Teaching activities are defined as all those actions of students and teachers in the classroom. There are many dozens of possible activities that can be organized into several categories.

Verbal   Hear

Visual △ **See**

Simulated   Identify With

Direct Experiences   Do

Verbal Activities: lecture, discussion, recording, sermon, story, reading, and any other verbal presentation that depends primarily upon the hearing of the learner. There is evidence that most people do not learn well by hearing only. In order to be effective, other types of experiences must accompany verbal activities. Hearing is very selective. We tend to hear what we want to hear.

Visual Symbols: use of teaching pictures, filmstrips, studying, seeing movies, looking at books, and many other types visual presentations. Seeing is less passive than hearing. Seeing elicits a response from the one who sees. When verbal and visual symbols are used together in a combined activity, the learning is more effective than when either is used separately.

Simulated Experience: role playing, dramatics, simulated games, some field trips, some creative writing and other experiences that place students in the position of acting out particular feelings, problems, or issues.

Direct Experiences: are those activities when students are actually involved in "for real' situation, problems, and concepts. Because so many concepts in religious teaching tend to be abstract it is often difficult to design direct experience teaching activities.

Deciding which teaching activity/method to use is the necessary task all teachers must perform. Here are some criteria that may be used in deciding which teaching activities to employ:

1. The activity should involve most of the students in an active way.
2. It should be an activity in which the teacher has some confidence.
3. It should allow for maximum creativity on the part of the student.
4. It should not be so familiar as to bore the students.
5. It is a new activity, students should have opportunity to experiment with it in order to discover its possibilities.
6. There should usually be a variety of activities offered so that the students can have a choice.
7. The activity should contribute directly to communicating the key concept and achieving the specific objectives.
8. The activities should lead the students to seek answers, state conclusions or express creative responses.
9. Whatever activities are designed should be appropriate to the ages and skills of the students involved.

Teachers always need to be alert to new ways of designing activities. By reading, sharing, and experiencing a variety of activities teachers will become more resourceful in their planning and teaching.

Disciples Make Disciples Who Make Disciples Who Make Disciples

Teachers can use a variety of techniques. They can ask questions, present lectures, facilitate creative learning experiences, or use a number of other teaching methods. The point, however, is not what the teacher does. **It is what happens inside the learner as a result of what the teacher does.** Regardless of one's teaching technique, these seven things must take place for disciple-making learning to happen:

I. The Disciple Making, Learning Process
1. The learner must become interested in the lesson.
2. Truth must become truth that matters to the learner.
3. The learner must discover how this truth relates to Monday morning.
4. The learner must recognize the gap between his/her life and the life God calls us to live.
5. The learner must see the benefits of obedience and the drawbacks of disobedience.
6. The learner must commit to exchange one belief, value, attitude, or behavior for another.
7. The learner must be held accountable for his/her decisions and commitments.

II. Objectives: Fully Devoted Follower
- 1st base = membership
- 2nd base = maturity
- 3rd base = ministry
- home plate – multiplication

Reverend Dr. Anthony Jones

Steps in Lesson Preparation

1.   Begin with prayer as the center of the preparation.

2.   Read the text

   - Spend time reading from the Bible, not the
     quarterly. Use different versions and translations.
   - Read the entire passage, not just the focal
     passage.
   - Make notes (names, places, etc.)
   - Reread the passage, asking yourself these
     questions: What do these words mean?
     What do they mean to me?
     How do they apply to me?

3.   Identify the central truth of the passage.
   - Helps to bring the entire passage into focus
   - Write the central truth as you see it.
   - Use the present tense. It is not what did it mean,
     but what does it mean for us.

4.   Relate the lesson to the unit.

5.   Read the pupils' material.

6.   Use study helps.

   - Basic resources needed: a one-volume
     commentary; brief into to each book; outline;
     helps in interpretation
   - Bible concordance
   - Bible dictionary
   - Maps

7.   Consider needs of class members.

8.   Select truths to be emphasized.

9.   Decide on teaching methods.

10.   Make lesson plans.

- Keep all lesson plans.
- Put enough material in the lesson plan to do a last minute Bible study.
- Unit goal: What should students understand about this unit at the end of the unit?
- Lesson goal: What should students understand at the end of the lesson? What is the aim?
- Lesson objectives: Steps taken to reach the goals.

Suggested Lesson Preparation Schedule

SUNDAY:
- A. Begin early!
- B. Pray to God, asking Him to be your teacher.
- C. Read entire passage in at least two translations of the Bible.
- D. As you read, write out questions you may have.

MONDAY:
- A. Pray for prospects of whom have visited the class.
- B. Read background material from quarterly.
- C. Begin consulting Bible dictionary and other study tools.
- D. State the central truth of the lesson.
   - a. Key scriptural principle of the passage.
   - b. State it in the present tense form.
   - c. Write it out (one or two sentences).

TUESDAY:
- A. Pray for class members.
- B. Visit members and prospects.
- C. Read other commentaries.
- D. Consider the needs and possible learning goals for the lesson.

WEDNESDAY:
- A. Pray for Sunday School and/ or Department Director.
- B. Attend Weekly Workers 'Meeting.
- C. Look through the Resource Kit.
- D. Look at suggested teaching procedure (teacher's quarterly).

THURSDAY:
- A. Pray for members by name.
- B. Clarify the teaching goal.
- C. Write out the teaching aim.
- D. Read the Biblical Illustrator articles.

    E. Brainstorm possible learning activities.
    F. Pray for members by name.
    G. Clarify the teaching goal.
    H. Write out the teaching aim.
    I.   Read the Biblical Illustrator articles.
    J. Brainstorm possible learning activities.

FRIDAY:
    A. Pray for the lesson plan development.
    B. Read through the scripture passage again.
    C. Write out learning activities.

SATURDAY:

    A. Pray for Pastor and Staff.
    B. Fill out detailed lesson plan (Step 1, Step 2, ...)
    C. Rehearse in your mind how to progress from step to step.
    D. Gather materials for lesson.

The Lesson Cycle

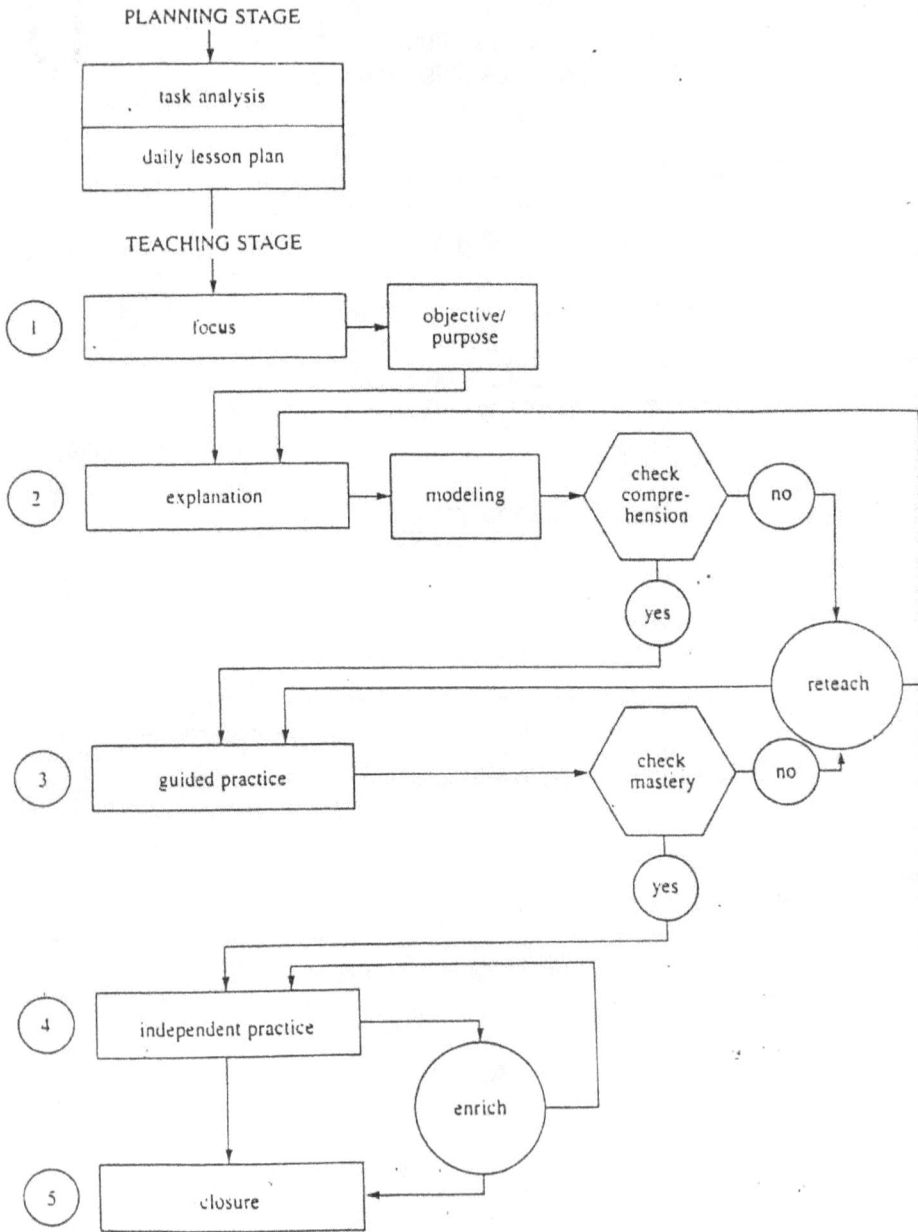

Using the Lesson Teaching Sequences

The five steps of an effective lesson plan are shown below and developed in detail in the description of The Lesson Cycle, which follows.

Step 1

- Focus
- Objective

Step 2

- Explanation
- Modeling
- Check for knowledge and comprehension

Step 3

- Guided practice
- Check mastery
- Re-teach

Step 4

- Independent practice
- Enrichment

Step 5

- Closure

The Lesson Cycle

The Planning Stage

The lesson cycle is a teacher decision-making process involving lesson content, teacher behavior, and learner behavior. The first stage of the lesson cycle is the planning stage. This stage includes the task analysis, in which teachers select the objectives at the appropriate level and identify the prescribed elements of curriculum being taught. Next, the teacher will plan the daily lesson, incorporating the appropriate teaching steps into the instructional design.

The Teaching Stage

The second stage is the teaching stage. This stage uses the five-step lesson plan.

Step One

Focus generates student interest in the learning that is to follow. The focus, often referred to as the anticipatory set, should involve the learner in a relevant way and develop student readiness for the instruction to follow. The focus should also connect past instruction to the current instruction with a technique called transfer. Other techniques of focus include asking divergent questions, role playing, telling stories or anecdotes, showing pictures and cartoons, and using inquiry methods.

Objective/Purpose tells students what they will be able to do by the end of the instruction. The objective also states why learning is important, useful, and relevant for the student.

Step Two

Explanation is the method selected by the teacher to present the objective (information) to students. Techniques may include the use of definitions, rules, process steps, and examples.

Modeling is what the teacher does to cause the learner to see or to imitate the learning. Modeling allows the learning process to be demonstrated visually. Techniques include giving both visual and oral demonstrations, showing examples of an acceptable finished product (story, poem, model, diagram, and graph), and identifying a process, such as throwing a football or kicking a soccer ball.

Checking for knowledge and comprehension is what the teacher does to assess student understanding of the learning. Techniques include posing key questions to students and asking them to explain concepts, definitions, and attributes in their own words.

Monitoring and adjusting is the process of observing the learning environment and the learner behavior during instruction and, if necessary, changing the instruction to achieve the desired results.

Step Three

Guided practice is student practice monitored by the teacher. The teacher can guide the student through the problem, skill, or work to be done and can provide feedback to the student.

Re-teaching occurs when learning has not taken place or when students have not mastered the objectives

Step Four

Independent practice is student practice without teacher assistance. In evaluating the appropriate amount of practice, two psychological principles should be taken into consideration.
- Massing practice at the beginning speeds up learning.
- Distributing practice after material is learned improves retention.

New material should be practiced briefly, intensely, and frequently. As the material becomes internalized, practice should become less frequent and should be spaced farther and farther apart.

Enrichment occurs after learning has taken place, following guided and independent practice. Knowledge is extended with higher-level activities.

Step Five

Closure is bringing the lesson to a logical conclusion. The teacher will involve students by letting them summarize what they have learned in their own words. Do not end a lesson without bringing closure.

Sample Lesson

Bold Faith-Mark 7:24-37

Planning Stage:
Use the following tools to plan your lesson; commentaries (Standard Sunday School Commentary, Sunday School teacher's guide, Matthew Henry commentary, Life Application Bible study notes and Echoes), read all of the **devotional readings** for the week, read the **chapters** before/after the text. Read and study every day.

Step One:
Focus: We need to intercede for others. Ask your students to think about the adults whom they thought were great "prayer warriors" during their childhood. Ask them to identify one of them and briefly describe his/her impact on them. What did this person regularly pray for? When your class is ready to begin, remind your students that as Christians we have an obligation to pray for other people and to be strong in our faith when their faith may be weak.

Discuss why Christians should be willing to intercede for others (read story on page 68, then form small groups to discuss).

Transfer: (Link to Last week): Ask the incoming students if they were able to do any extra ordinary tasks for Christ during the past week.

State Objective/Purpose:
➤ Considers how to intercede for others and what happens in intercession.
➤ Intercede for people who need God's help.

Step Two:
Explanation: You must make the lesson relevant to the students. Try to emphasize 3-5 important points that you want them to remember and apply to their lives. Use definitions, examples, demonstrations, role-playing, stories, games, interviews, computers, video tapes, or poems to explain:
Part I:
Mark 7:24-30- A Woman Presents Her Case
Part II:
Mark 7:31-37-Friends Intercede for a Deaf and Mute Man

Step Three:
Application Activities: Get the Students Involved!

➤ A Parable about Prayer-Write a script for a parable that illustrates the power of prayer in terms of interceding for someone who needs Christ's aid. It could be a health issue, a life-threatening situation, or a spiritual crisis. The group could act out the parable.

➤ Use the word PRAY as an acronym for this exercise. Come up with as many words as you can think of that identify the type of people you should pray for and whose first letter matches a letter in the word PRAY (for example, P=Poor, R=Rulers, A=Ailing, Y=Youth).

➤ When We Intercede-Write next to each day a person you intend to intercede for. During the week, share prayer requests about the people you are praying for and write that news after their names:
Monday- _____
Tuesday-_____
Wednesday- _____
Thursday-   _____
Friday-   _____
Saturday-   _____
Sunday-   _____

Step Four-Closure:

➤ End the class with a final prayer. As you pray, ask God to help specific people for whom your students feel particularly burdened. Thank God that He not only listens to our prayers but also answers them in a way that is best for the people we pray for.

➤ Class Assignment: Mark 8:27-9:13-Ask your student for the next class session to think about incidents in their lives that helped them comprehend fully who Jesus is.

The 22 Deadly Sins of Lesson Presentation

1. Appearing Unprepared
This does not mean that you actually are unprepared; it simply means that you seem to be. Examples of an appearance of unpreparedness would be not being able to locate your next transparency or not knowing what comes next unless you have your notes right in front of you. A presenter who appears unprepared runs the risk of appearing unqualified to be presenting.

2. Starting Late
Whether everyone is there or not, start on time. Otherwise, we penalize those who are on time and reward those who are late. Be on time yourself and on time for the instructor means early. One rule of thumb is that you should be present and smiling at least 15 minutes prior to class starting. Another rule of thumb: Interact with your class members when the class is over.

3. Handling Questions Improperly
This means putting off questions, perhaps abruptly, by saying something like "I'll be covering that in a little while. Please wait until then," or combining questions: "Those two questions are somewhat similar, so I'll just answer them together." Or giving people the impression that there is an awkward question, or a question that didn't need to be asked. All these are examples of improper handling of questions.

4. Apologizing for Yourself or the Organization
If there's a problem, in all likelihood 80 percent of your students won't be aware of it. Take care of the people for whom there is a problem on an individual basis.

5. Being Unfamiliar with knowable Information
For example, not knowing the names of the key leaders and not knowing the name of the organization to which you're making a presentation.

6. Using Audio Visuals Unprofessionally
This includes things like not knowing how to operate the slide projector or showing poorly prepared transparencies. As audiences become increasingly sophisticated, they expect not only to be able

to read any visuals used, but also ensure that those visuals are interesting enhancements to your presentation.

7. Seeming to be Off Schedule
In your introduction, you may have indicated that you are going to cover ten things in a one-day presentation. By lunch, you've covered two of them. Now, in your own mind you know that's exactly where you're supposed to be, because those two points provide the major base for the other eight that you'll introduce in the remaining time. But unless you explain that timeframe, your audience will assume that five points should have been covered before lunch and five after. As far as they're concerned, you're way behind, and you're probably going to cram a lot of information into the afternoon session. In order not to appear off schedule, tell participants where you're going and how long it's going to take to get there.

8. Not Involving the Students
The more you can involve people in the learning process, the more effective that learning is going to be. Adults bring experiences and expertise to your presentations. Take advantage of what the students bring to the presentation.

9. Not Establishing Personal Rapport
Simple ways to develop personal rapport are making and maintaining eye contact. Always try to be available 15 minutes before the start of a presentation, 15 minutes after the end of a presentation, and for at least half of any scheduled break.

10. Ending Late
This is even worse than starting late. I've never yet known a group of students that was pleased when a training program, a lesson, or presentation ran over the scheduled time. A guideline I use is to begin tying things together 15 minutes before the end of a presentation. This means I not only finish on schedule but I have time for a solid wrap-up that gives a sense of closure to the process.

11. Appearing Disorganized
You appear disorganized when you don't properly introduce things, you don't provide logical transitions from one part of your presentation to the next, and/or you don't summarize what you've been talking about. Remember: Tell them what you're going to tell them, and then tell them what you've told them.

12. Not Quickly Establishing a Positive Image

At the beginning of most presentations, people need some time to get focused and to get themselves going. Nevertheless, that's difficult if the person making the presentation also needs to take time to get focused and get going. Get started quickly by introducing a vivid illustration and by involving the group by asking questions. If you quickly take command, you give people the impression that you know who you are, where you are, and where you're going and that it is going to be exciting and fun for them to come along.

Actually, you establish an image of yourself and your program even before you open your mouth, by the look and feel of the materials that informed them of the program, by the handouts and manuals they received as they registered, by the type of facility in which the program is conducted, and by how you, as the instructor, are dressed. I believe we ought to dress just a little more formally than our participants expect. It's better to be a bit overdressed and make ourselves more casual by removing a jacket. We show participants respect by the way we dress.

13. Not Covering the Objectives Promised

In every class, there will be someone who checks very carefully to see that everything that has been promised has been delivered. "Promise much, deliver more." I agree. First, though, we must make sure that we deliver what we promised and then give the value-added material, the unexpected extras that can boost the program's success.

14. Not Scheduling Enough Breaks

Everybody may not be as fascinated with the subject as we are. But even the most interested student can only concentrate for so long. We need to let people stretch and move around. These mini-breaks allow for some stretching and walking activities.

15. Practicing Bad Habits

Check this one by videotaping yourself periodically to pick up on bad habits that may have crept into your presentation style. Do you: absentmindedly jingle change, lean on the lectern as you present, or keep your hands in your pockets too much? Do you punctuate your delivery with non-words, such as "um" or "er"? Practice should help eliminate these verbal ticks. Getting rid of distracting habits and mannerisms can enhance the effectiveness of our presentations.

16. Not Checking the Environment
Avoid this by diligently checking- and checking yet again-all elements of the presentation setting: room setups, temperature, light, sound, equipment, and all materials, you'll use yourself and distribute to students.

17. Not Updating Material
Students expect us to be current, and we should be. As teachers of the word, we cannot become complacent with what we have. We must constantly be looking for ways to involve the students and bring new material.

18. Not Admitting Mistakes
As presenters, we are not perfect: we make mistakes, and we do not have all the answers. When we do not know an answer or we do make a mistake, we must admit it either to an individual or, if appropriate, to the entire group.

19. Using Inappropriate Humor
Any humor that offends or makes fun of any student is inappropriate and will kill your presentation.

20. Using Inappropriate Language
Be careful what you say, you may offend your audience and run them off forever.

21. Coming on As an Expert, a Know-it-all
Most of us study our Bibles and commentaries. But our teaching shouldn't be flaunted to the point that it makes students feel small. Our advanced knowledge hardly makes us superior human beings.

22. Using Poor Grammar, Pronunciation, and Enunciation
Don't let participants think, "How you say it sounds so awful that I can't hear what you say."

APPENDIX

**The purpose of every
presentation is to persuade.**

What is your goal? Your objective?

What do you want to accomplish?

The key to achieving your goal is...

Learning Retention Scale

We retain.......

90% Do	
70% Say	
50% See/Hear	
30 % See	
10% Hear	

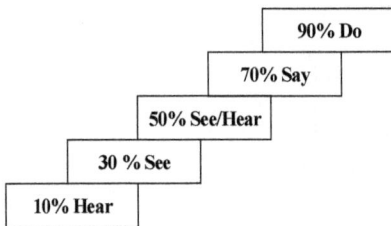

Learner retention
increases in direct
proportion to learner
participation.......

Preparation!

Using Handouts

Do's

- Ensure handouts are double-spaced and one-sided.
- Proofread for errors in grammar and spelling before copying.
- Make sure handouts clearly and correctly reflect what you want the audience to remember.
- Decide ahead of time how and when you want them distributed.
- Number pages and label charts/graphs for easy reference.
- Label with your name, date, and topic so participants will recall when
  and why they received them.
- Give credit where credit is due.
- Use different colors for different topics.
- Make sure copies are clean and legible.
- Make more copies than you need.
- Use corresponding overheads to keep the group with you.
- Use an editor's blue pencil to keep originals separate from copies.

Don'ts

- Don't give a truckload when a bale of hay is enough!
- Highlight handouts after copying. Highlighters (except yellow) generally don't copy well and may block out the words you wanted emphasized. If you want to highlight prior to copying, underline.
- Avoid blue felt-tip pens for items to be copied. Black, red, or green photocopy more clearly.

Using Flip Charts

Do's
- Plan presentation/points on notepaper.
- Use manuscript, not cursive writing.
- Keep it simple, using color and varied lettering to emphasize points.
- Keep print in proportion to page size.
- Write pages on pad in the order you will use them.
- Use lettering guide's -2 inches for 30 feet; 4 inches for 60 feet; beyond that, go to another medium.
- Make notes to yourself in pencil.
- Leave 1-2 blank pages between sheets to avoid "bleed through."
- Use paper clips or numbered tabs on edges of pages to easily locate and flip to desired page.
- Position for your ease of use and audience visibility.
- **PRACTICE** turning pages so you can do it smoothly and quietly.
- Always have your own markers with you.

Don'ts
- Turn to one side of room
- Turn your back to audience and talk to chart stand
- Stand in front of chart while pointing

Checklist
- Is there enough paper?
- Are marking pens available and not dried out?
- Is there masking tape for posting sheets?

Using Chalkboards

Do's

- Write large enough for all to see.
- Use manuscript rather than cursive.
- Use yellow chalk for optimal visibility.
- Use worn chalk rather than brand new. New sticks break easily and the resulting small pieces screech on the board.
- Avoid getting chalk dust on your clothes.
- Erase as you go, using damp cloth so when you need to reuse a space it will be dry.
- Have your own box of chalk with you.

Don'ts

- Talk with your back to the audience.
- Gesture or fumble with the chalk. Put it down on the ledge when you are through with your point.

Using Technology

Do's

- Practice, practice, practice ahead.
- Show up early and test all equipment.
- Have back-up equipment.
- Have back-up materials should all equipment fail.
- Have confidence in what you are doing.

Don'ts

- Attempt to "razzle-dazzle" if you aren't familiar and comfortable with approach.
- Fail, if equipment fails. Smoothly resort to back-up plan.

<u>You</u>

- Preparation

- Visual: How you look

- Verbal: What you say

- Vocal: How you sound

<u>Visual/Verbal/Vocal</u>

- Visual 55%

- Verbal 12%

- Vocal 33%

Remember....

People <u>see</u> you before they <u>hear</u> you!

<u>Visual</u>

<u>Nonverbal</u>
- Eye contact
- Facial expressions
- Head movements
- Gestures
- Posture
- Dress

Avoid

- Swaying/rocking motion
- Pacing
- Staring at floor, ceiling, notes
- Jingling coins in pockets
- Pointing finger at audience
- Slumping, slouching shoulders
- Distracting, unprofessional dress
- Distracting hand actions

Vocal

Control

-too high/low

- natural and relaxed
- interesting and expressive

-too loud/soft

- volume inconsistent
- room size/audience size

-too fast/slow

- monotonous
- unnatural

Relax...Be Confident, JUST DO IT!

Reverend Dr. Anthony Jones

Additional Notes

Additional Notes

Reverend Dr. Anthony Jones

Additional Notes

Additional Notes

ABOUT THE AUTHOR

***

Rev. Dr. Anthony Jones has a tremendous passion for God's word coupled with a love for God's people. He has a contagious spirit of generosity that flows through every facet of his ministry. Having received his mandate from God, Dr. Jones, obediently fulfills his calling as a Minister of GOD's word.

Called to ministry in January of 2003, under the leadership of Dr. Airon Reynolds Jr., Pastor of Borden Chapel Missionary Baptist Church.

His mission is uncompromisingly clear, with one central principle; to build and develop a kingdom of empowered people for God. Holding firmly to the commissioned mandate in Matthew 28:18-20, *"Go ye therefore, and teach all nations"*, Dr. Jones has taken the gospel into national and international communities of the world.

Dr. Jones received his Doctorate of Divinity and Doctorate of Theology degree from Oval Bible College and his Masters of Theology from Oval Bible College. He received his Bachelor of Science in Management from Jacksonville State University.

DORINV PUBLICATIONS

www.ingramcontent.com/pod-product-compliance
Lightning Source LLC
Chambersburg PA
CBHW071435040426
42445CB00012BA/1367